ABOVE: *The Old Flowerpot Inn at Kingswood, Avon.*

INN SIGNS

Cadbury Lamb

Shire Publications Ltd

CONTENTS

Printed in Great Britain by City Print (Milton Keynes) Ltd, Denbigh Hall, Bletchley, Bucks.

This book is based upon *Discovering Inn Signs* by Cadbury Lamb and Gordon Wright, published in 1968.

The Bee Hive, Abingdon, Oxon.

THE BEE HIVE

Within this hive we're all alive,
Good liquor makes us funny,
If you are dry step in and try
the flavour of our honey.

MORLAND

The famous sign of Ye Olde Starre Inne spans Stanegate in York.

THE ORIGINS OF INN SIGNS

No one knows who put up the first shop sign but the practice first appears common among the Romans, and at Pompeii signs have been found depicting draught or chequer boards, which were the emblems of money lenders. The Roman sign of a tavern was a bush of vine leaves, the origin of the saying 'a good wine needs no bush', and a few brewers still continue the practice of hanging up a bunch of evergreen – an ale garland – at the opening of a new house.

At a time when very few people were literate, signs were the only way of proclaiming one's trade and as communities became more sophisticated so did the need for some sort of advertisement. All traders used signs, not just innkeepers, and as competition increased so the signs became more elaborate, often reaching right across the street, but after the Great Fire of London, Charles II decreed that signs should in future be fixed against the walls or balconies of houses. But signs continued to become larger and more decorative and in 1712 one fell down in Fleet Street, pulling the front of the house with it and killing four people.

Inns offered both refreshment and accommodation, and some of the earliest inns in Britain were built to accommodate pilgrims, who were the largest single group of medieval travellers. Hostels for them were built at abbeys and pilgrimage centres and, understandably, were distinguished by religious signs.

One of the most famous of these is *The George and Pilgrims* at Glastonbury, which accommodated travellers

3

The Cross Keys at King's Cliffe, Northants, and The Angel at Corbridge, Northumberland, are both religious signs from the days of medieval pilgrims.

who came to see the relics at the abbey. Others are *The Star*, Alfriston, East Sussex, and *The Manor of God Begot*, Winchester. *The Trout* at Godstow, near Oxford, stands on the site of the hostel for Godstow nunnery.

The influence of the church and of pilgrims was such that many inns used religious references as their signs: *Crossed Keys* were the insignia of Saint Peter; *The Lamb* is often a reference to Christ; *Angel, Adam and Eve, Abbey* and *Mitre* have obvious religious origins; *The Salutation* refers to the Annunciation; and *The Bull* is often a corruption of *bulla*, the Latin for a monastic seal, which would have been put up on many inns owned by the local abbey. *The Anchor* was a religious sign as much as a maritime one, and *The Ship* often appears represented as the Ark. There is a *Noah's Ark* at St Albans, Herts.

Saints receive numerous mentions. Saint George is the most popular in England, and the sign *The George* on many inns is often a corruption of Saint George and the Dragon. *The Catherine Wheel* at Crowell, Oxon, has a grim representation of martyrdom. This was a popular sign because it was the badge of the Knights of Saint Catherine of Mount Sinai, created in the eleventh century for the protection of pilgrims on their way to Jerusalem. There is a record of such a sign in London being changed by Cromwell's iconoclasts to *The Cat and Wheel*. Similarly many *Salutation* inns became *Soldier and Citizen*, only to revert to their original name on the Restoration.

The influence of the Holy Land and the Crusades is still very marked on our inn signs - *The Turk's Head* or *The Saracen's Head*, and one inn claimed to be the oldest in England, *The Trip to Jerusalem* in Nottingham. *The Lamb and Flag*, from the coat of arms of the Knights Templar, partly originated from the idea of the Lamb of God. The same device appears on the arms of the Merchant Taylors, and some inns may have taken their name from this.

Around North Marston, Bucks, are several inns called *The Boot*, which is a reference to the feat of the rector, Sir John Shorn, who in the thirteenth century is claimed to have conjured the Devil into a boot.

4

This unusual carved sign at Cley-next-the-Sea in Norfolk is an example of Saint George and the Dragon being corrupted to The George.

ROYAL AND HERALDIC SIGNS

After the Church, the most powerful influence upon the development of inn signs was the monarchy, as the many *Crowns* and *King's Heads* show. The reasons are obvious. Many of our inns date back to times when the royal succession was anything but certain, and anyone proclaiming his trade as obviously as a publican had to be sure of keeping in with the authorities. During the Wars of the Roses keepers of *King's Head* inns and *Rose* inns must have been continually changing the face of the monarch or the colour of the rose on their signs, and no doubt many changed over to the less specific *Crown* in the hope of pleasing anyone who happened to be wearing it at the time.

The crest of Richard III was a white boar and became a popular sign during his reign. After his death keepers of *White Boars* must have blessed the Earl of Oxford, whose crest was a blue boar, for supporting Henry Tudor. They had only to paint the boar blue to show a healthy respect for the new reign. *The Blue Boar* at North Heath, Berks, however, gets its name from the 'stone pig' left behind by Cromwell's soldiers.

A consequence of the marriage of Henry VII to Elizabeth of York, daughter of Edward IV, was a rash of *Rose and Crowns,* many of which still survive.

The Crown was often the name of an inn which stood on royal property and,

5

The Lamprey at Gloucester has royal associations. Henry I died from eating too many.

a pure white stag and placed a gold collar round its neck. The collared hart was also adopted by Henry V and Edward IV.

The heraldic figures supporting the royal arms changed with the accession of James I. The unicorn of Scotland was one of them and gave rise to many inn signs. The Hanoverians brought with them the Saxon emblem, the white horse.

On the accession of Charles II a forest of *Royal Oaks* sprouted all over England. The sign commemorates Charles's escape from the Parliamentary army by hiding in an oak tree at Boscobel. *The Royal Standard of England* at Forty Green, Bucks, claims to have received its name from Charles II for sheltering him during his escape.

Just as inns on royal land publicised their allegiance to the Crown so inns on manorial lands supported the local baron. Complete coats of arms are familiar on inn signs but some signs use a symbol only. *The Red Lion,* so popular still, was the sign of John of Gaunt; *The Bear and Ragged Staff* was the crest of the powerful Earls of Warwick; *The Eagle and Child* was that of the Stanleys, Earls of Derby; *The White Bear* the Earls of Kent; *The Green Dragon* the Earls of Pembroke; *The Swan* the Dukes of Buckingham; *The Talbot* the Earls of Shrewsbury; *The Eagle* the Earls of Cambridge; *The Wheatsheaf* the Earls of Exeter; *The White Horse* the Earls of Arundel.

This practice of naming inns after the local landowners continued long after the Middle Ages. Around Aylesbury, Bucks, the Rothschild family built several mansions at the end of the last century and the *Rothschild Arms* is a familiar sign, while the *Five Arrows* at Waddesdon refers to part of the family's coat of arms representing the five sons in the family.

A survey of 19,000 British inn names by G. W. Shearn of Northampton lists the most popular names as follows: *Red Lion* (386 examples), *Crown* (350), *White Hart* (269), *New* (234), *King's Head* (178), *King's Arms* (159), *Royal Oak* (151).

as the monarch was one of the biggest landowners in the country, this is another reason for the prevalence of the sign. The variation *Three Crowns* refers to the uniting of the three kingdoms under James I. At Devizes the sign is depicted as three coins.

Most kings of England have used the lion on their coat of arms but Edward III used a rising sun and this may be the origin of many signs of that name that still exist. Later, when Edward claimed the throne of France, he incorporated the French emblem – the fleur de lys – into his arms and innkeepers followed his lead. Sometimes this became altered to a plume of feathers after Edward's son, the Black Prince, adopted the feathers as his badge, although ostrich plumes were borne by English kings as long ago as Stephen. At Princes Risborough, Bucks, where the Prince's palace once stood, is a sign *The Black Prince.*

But the most popular sign taken from a monarch's arms comes from the Black Prince's son Richard II. He used a swan and an antelope with a collar and the latter has become the ubiquitous *White Hart.* The origin of this creature goes back to Alexander the Great who is supposed to have caught

6

WHITE HART

The Bear, Oxford, has its ragged staff, the crest of the Earls of Warwick and of Elizabeth's Earl of Leicester.

The White Hart in Old Woking refers to the legend in which Alexander the Great captured a white stag and placed a collar of gold around its neck.

The Red Lion at Martlesham, Suffolk, used a ship's figurehead as its sign.

The Swan at Clare, Suffolk, has a finely carved sign.

THE FISH

Snooty Fox

A ferocious pike looks over the street at Sutton Court-
enay in Oxon. The Snooty Fox is at Tetbury, Gloucestershire. The Black Dog in Weymouth, Dorset, recalls a
local story. The White Hart at Uppingham, Leicestershire,
has a finely executed sign. The Cat and Fiddle Inn, near
Buxton, is the second highest pub in England.

BLACK DOG

WHITE HART

The Fox and Hounds gallows sign at Barley, Herts.

ANIMAL SIGNS

Although many signs that depict animals have their origins in heraldry large numbers have other derivations. *The Bear,* a sign often associated with the Earls of Warwick and Leicester, is also a reference to the bear-baiting that often took place in inn yards. Many of these changed to *The Bull* when the fashion changed from bear- to bull-baiting, and other inns were named after that other vicious sport, cock-fighting. *The Fighting Cocks* at St Albans, Herts, is one of the oldest inns in England.

In Stony Stratford, Bucks, stand *The Cock* and *The Bull,* two old coaching inns whose competition for trade gave rise to the phrase 'a cock and bull story'.

Hunting accounts for many animal signs – *The Fox and Hounds, The Dog and Badger, The Hare and Hounds,* *The Stag and Hounds, The Fox's Brush* (at Grantham), *The Dog and Pheasant, The Dog and Duck.* But although Soho in London derives its name from a hunting call, *The Intrepid Fox* there is named after the politician Charles James Fox.

It is to be expected that many country pubs should be called after farm stock, and there are hundreds of *Cows* – dun, brown, spotted and even crazy. The sign *Lamb* often has a religious meaning, and *The Goat and Compasses* is sometimes thought to be a corruption of 'God encompasses us'. Horses are mostly connected with farming or racing. *The Suffolk Punch* in Ipswich pin-points a local breed and there are *Grey Mares* around Widecombe in Devon. *The Sow and Pigs* at Wadesmill, Herts, refers to a popular eighteenth-century card game.

9

The Horse and Tiger at Thorpe Hesley near Rotherham is said to refer to an accident when a tiger in a travelling menagerie broke loose and attacked the horses pulling a stagecoach.

Most British wild animals have inns named after them. A unique one is *The Polecat* at Prestwood, Bucks, although the origin of this is, in fact, the name of past lords of the manor, the Policates. *The Badger Box* at Annesley, Notts, recalls a chained badger at the inn used for fighting Cairn terriers.

Foreign animals are less common unless of heraldic origin. *The Elephant and Castle,* sometimes said to be a corruption of Infanta de Castile, is the crest of the Cutlers' Company, but *The Elephant's Nest* at Tavistock, Devon, and *The Blue Monkey,* Plymouth, defy explanation. *The Bear* at Box, Wilts, is a koala.

Among birds *The Cock, The Eagle* and *The Swan* are the commonest. *The Swan with Two Necks* refers to the practice of nicking the bills during swan-upping. The game birds come next in frequency and *The Falcon, The Hawk and Duck,* and *The Bird in Hand* refer to the ancient sport of hawking. *The Sparrow Hawk* at Edgware recalls the granting of the manor by the Countess of Salisbury to her son for the annual payment of one sparrow hawk.

The Pelican appears by virtue of its supposed devotion to its young, and

This carved sign at Devizes, Wilts, shows a bear carrying a bunch of grapes in its mouth. Opposite is the Black Bull at Sleaford, Lincs, with a bull-baiting plaque alongside the sign.

pelicans were used to symbolise the Virgin Mary. An occasional inn has been called the Pelican because of the size of its 'bill'. *The Dove,* the religious emblem of peace, is popular for this reason. *The Peacock* also has ancient symbolism. Its flesh was considered incorruptible, and the phrase 'by the Peacock' became a popular oath.

Cats appear on many signs, like *The Cat and Fiddle* at Hinton Admiral, Dorset, and the one on the lonely moorland road between Buxton and Macclesfield, which stands nearly 1,700 feet above sea-level. At Windley Meadows is *The Puss in Boots,* with an attractive rhyming verse. In north London, at Highgate Hill, is a *Whittington and Cat;* at Colwick, Notts, there is a *Ginger Tom,* whilst Shipton Moyne, Wilts, boasts, perhaps, the most unusual of the entire species, *The Cat and Custard Pot* which, on the less literal side of the signboard, depicts a hunt meet involving Mr John Jorrocks, MFH, that well-known sporting character of R. S. Surtees.

Ducks have many pubs named after them. Near the famous Wildfowl Trust property at Slimbridge, Glos, is *The Wild Duck* at Ewen. There is a *Drunken Duck* at Barngate, Cumbria, and a *Whistling Duck* at Banwell, Avon, the name of which came from an eight-year-old girl who won the competition organised by the brewers to find the most original title for this new inn. Of course, Aylesbury has a *Duck.* There is a *Gaping Goose* at Oldham, and *The Bullfinch* at Riverhead, Kent.

Waterside inns are often named after fish. *The Trout* is probably the most popular. At Staverton, Devon, there is a *Sea Trout.* At Mepal, Cambs, is *The Three Pickerels. The Three Fishes* is heraldic in origin, so is *The Three Frogs* at Wokingham, Berks.

Insects are not common, except perhaps *Bees* and *The Beehive.* At Grantham the sign is an actual beehive in a tree outside the pub. In Harlow New Town the pubs have been named after butterflies – *Purple Emperor, White Admiral, Essex Skipper,* and *Garden Tiger.*

THE ROW BARGE

THE SILENT WHISTL

The Row Barge at Guildford stands by the river Wey. The Silent Whistle at Evercreech, Somerset, was called The Railway Hotel before the station was closed. The Bristol Flyer in Gloucester Road, Bristol, recalls a famous coach. The Toll House near Bridport, Dorset, is a reminder of the days when traffic using turnpikes had to pay for their upkeep.

TOLL HOUSE

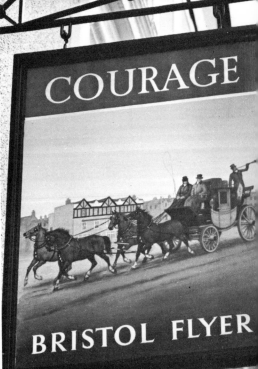

COURAGE

BRISTOL FLYER

This unusual sign, showing an attractive four-wheeled carriage used in Malta, is at Preston, near Oakham, Leicestershire.

SIGNS OF TRAVEL

Inns being places of refreshment for travellers, it is not surprising that a great number retain in their signs some reference to the business of getting from one place to another. When public transport was non-existent few people travelled for pleasure; the main reason was trade, and the simplest method was by foot – as in *The Pedlar's Pack* and *The Running Footman,* Mayfair. *The Packhorse,* more common, as at Milton Hill, Oxon, and *The Woolpack* at Stoke Mandeville, Bucks, recall the usual method of transporting England's staple commodity, wool, across the country to the southern and eastern ports. *The Wagon and Horses* originates, not so much from the farmer carrying his wares to market, as from the local carrier who used inns as his points of delivery and collection.

It was, however, the coming of the stagecoach and the mail-coach that really changed the signs and the organisation of the English inn. The first stagecoaches appeared in the 1720s but progress depended very much upon the weather conditions and the ability of the passengers to push the vehicle out of any ruts into which it might fall, an eventuality illustrated on the sign of *Puesdown Inn,* Glos. With the development of turnpikes speeds improved and

the 'flying' coaches began to cover distances between the main cities at an average of ten miles per hour. By 1830 the Royal Mail coach to Bath was leaving London at 7.30 a.m. and arriving in Bath at 9 p.m. the same evening. The coaches bore fanciful names and their efficiency depended upon the changeover of horses at the various stages en route. So trained became the staff at the stage inns that horses were changed in two or three minutes and passengers were fed in fifteen. To service a fast coach at the peak of the coaching era at least one horse per mile of the journey was needed. Therefore inns had to have enormous stabling facilities and some of those on the Bath Road might have accommodation for up to two hundred horses.

With all this it is not surprising that we still find so many *Coach and Horses* inns, *Four-in-Hand, Horse and Groom* and *Three Horseshoes* (suggesting the loss of a shoe). Turnpikes are remembered by *The Gate, The Tollgate;* stopping places by *Halfway House;* and the arrival at destinations by *Journey's End* and *Rest and Be Thankful.*

Many inns are still named after the coaches that called. *The Royal Blenheim* at Oxford, *The Gloucester Flying Machine* near Gloucester, *The Quick-*

The Coach and Horses is a popular sign. This one at Chislehampton, Oxon, is thought to be the largest painted sign in the country. It is over eleven feet long and six feet wide and was painted in three sections. The coach is a copy of a mail-coach in the Science Museum in London.

silver Mail at East Coker in Somerset and *The Eclipse* at Tunbridge Wells are all names of coaches. *The Dairy Maid* in Aylesbury, however, is a recent public house named after the famous coach that brought to Aylesbury the news of the victory at Waterloo.

All this prosperity and organisation collapsed, however, with the coming of the railway. The effect was catastrophic. In the ten years from 1836 to 1846, passenger traffic moved from coach to train wherever the railway went. Turnpike receipts were halved, then halved again. Inns closed, towns that were once thriving became near derelict, and thousands of grooms, ostlers and coachmen found themselves out of work.

Where the railway was in close proximity the names of inns were changed to *Railway Hotel, Great Western, Locomotive;* elsewhere new inns were built at stations, forming the nucleus of new developments serving the railway and taking advantage of the trade that it brought.

The motorcar, however, is swinging the pendulum back again. As railways close, new roads are built and old roads improved, and the coaching inns that survived now enjoy revived fortunes. Railway inns are changing their names again, and those that do not are using their signs as historic records of *Puffing Billy, The Rocket, The Marlow Donkey* and other famous engines. At Amersham, Bucks, *The Iron Horse* by the Metropolitan underground station depicts an old locomotive on one side of its sign, and a modern electric train on the other.

The Satellite at Bletchley, Bucks, is a three-dimensional sign. At The Anchor at Yateley, Hants, an old sign has been given a new interpretation. The sign was unveiled in 1972 by Felix Pole, the balloonist. The Ship at Brancaster in Norfolk uses a model, about four feet high, as its sign.

The Smith's Arms at Godmanstone in Dorset is claimed to be the smallest lock-up pub.

TRADE SIGNS

Many trade signs own their origin to the fact that associations of tradesmen were in the habit of meeting in licensed houses and that trade unions often held their meetings in 'the local'. There are examples of various 'arms' all over Britain – well over a hundred different kinds, reflecting local industries (Hufflers, Scutchers, Slubbers, Pyrotechnists and Flintknappers) and ranging alphabetically from *The Auctioneer* at Measham, Leics, to *The Yarn Spinner* at Spondon, near Derby.

The Wheatsheaf, found in all wheat-growing counties, was formerly a baker's sign; three golden wheatsheaves appear in the arms of the Company of Bakers of London.

A 'flaming sword' was a favourite with Cutlers at one time, but a better-known connection with the Cutlers' Company (over five hundred years old) is *The Elephant and Castle*. Heraldically, the elephant was represented with a castle on his back (symbolising the howdah); possibly the Cutlers used this as their crest because the bone in knife-handles could sometimes be passed off as ivory!

The crest of the Company of Carpenters contained three compasses. As houses were formerly timber-built,

THE FROG

This public house at Tilehurst, Berks, was built upon the site of an old brickworks. 'Frog' is the name for the indentation of a brick. The sign depicts Beatrix Potter's character Jeremy Fisher.

Another Tilehurst pub with a humorous sign painted for Courage by the artist G. E. Mackenney.

FOX AND HOUNDS

builders were often called carpenters. Hence an inn would use *The Three Compasses* as a beckoning sign (as at Kingston in Greater London. *The Rabbits* at Stapleford Abbots, Essex, is a corruption of the carpentry term 'rebate'.

The Three Horseshoes (or sometimes *The Farriers' Arms*) represents the arms of the smiths, i.e. the London Company of Farriers (as at Ripley, Derbyshire). It also resembles the coat of arms of the Ferrers family, Earls of Derby, in the fourteenth century.

Noah's Ark (as at Derby and nearby Borrowash) is the crest of the London Company of Shipwrights. In coastal towns, the sign is found as *The Shipwrights' Arms.* In Chatham *The Hook and Hatchet* carries as a sign a copy of the badge of a Chief Petty Officer Shipwright – an allusion to the days when the navy had timber-felling rights to obtain wood for ship-building. *The Beetle and Wedge* at Moulsford, Oxon, is called after the tools used for splitting logs.

The Three Tuns (at Lichfield, Staffs, and elsewhere) is the arms of the Company of Vintners, incorporated in 1437. They also appear, on a chevron, in the arms of the Brewers' Company, granted about 1470.

The Ram is a sign with all kinds of variations and is often found in the Stroud valleys of Gloucestershire, long famous as a centre for the wool trade. It is the crest of the Drapers' Company, which dealt with cloth of all kinds. Closely associated with them were the Woolcombers, whose patron saint was Bishop Blaise and in whose honour inns can be found at Richmond, North Yorks, Andover, Hants, and Melton Mowbray, Leics. *The Fleece* and *Golden Fleece* also represent the wool trade.

SPORTING SIGNS

More than twenty sports are represented by inn names and inn signs: angling, archery, athletics, beagling, bowling, boxing, cricket, cycling, dog racing, fishing, football, golf, horse racing, hunting, pigeon racing, rowing, rugby, sailing, shooting, tennis and wrestling. In addition to all these, there are numerous references to ancient pastimes like cock-fighting, bear-baiting and falconry.

The Chequered Flag at Loddington, Northants, was so called when the New Inn became the headquarters of the Mid-Northants Car Club in 1963. In Derby there is a *Baseball Tavern,* in Leicester a *Speedway Tavern,* and at Sunderland an *Aquatic Arms. The Torch* at Wembley Park was opened shortly after the Olympic Games of 1948, held in Wembley Stadium: the sign depicts the arrival of the Olympic Torch.

There are over thirty pub names testifying to the popularity of cricket. One of the most attractive is the three-sided picture-sign *The Test Match* close by the famous Trent Bridge ground at Nottingham. At Hambledon, Hants, is *The Bat and Ball,* which claims to be the original home of the game. In London's Piccadilly, *The Yorker* features two giants of the past on its signboard. One is the redoubtable Dr W. G. Grace, quite easy to recognise; but what of the lean, saturnine figure in the striped blazer on the other side? This is F. R. Spofforth – 'The Demon' – who in the ninth Test between England and Australia in 1882 took fourteen wickets for ninety runs against the home country and so established the legend of the Ashes; he was six feet three inches in height and his yorker was virtually unplayable! *The Three Willows* at Birchanger in Essex shows the three different forms of the cricket bat as its pattern has changed

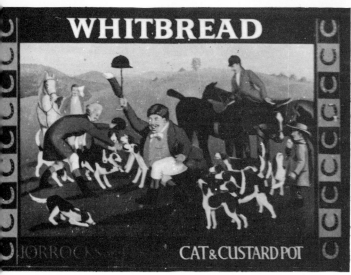

The two sides of The Yorker in Piccadilly, London, portray W. G. Grace and F. R. Spofforth, the bowler who originated the deadly yorker, which was considered virtually unplayable. The Cat and Custard Pot at Shipton Moyne in Wiltshire shows Surtees's character Jorrocks at a meeting of the hunt.

down the years. *The Maiden Over* in Reading depicts a girl leaping over a wicket.

Curiously enough, few signs refer to soccer, the most widely followed British game. Those named after League clubs in London are *The Gunners* at Finsbury Park (for Arsenal); *The Hammers* at West Ham; and *The Spurs* at Edmonton (for Tottenham Hotspur). Elsewhere we have *The Happy Wanderers* at Bolton, *The Saints* at Millbrook, Southampton, *United* in Ashton New Road, Manchester, and *The Sky Blue* at Coundon Green, Coventry, which refers to the local team's colour.

Many inns are named after racehorses: *Flying Childers* at Kirby Bellars, Leics, and at Stanton-in-the-Peak, Derbys; *The Flying Dutchman,* at Norwich, at Wombwell, near Barnsley, and at Hildenborough, Kent; *Master Robert* near Isleworth; *Old Spot* at Daybrook, near Nottingham, and *Little Wonder* at Harrogate. *The Starting Gate* at Newbury refers to the local racecourse.

Nottingham's renowned pugilist, William Abednego Thompson, is remembered by the inn bearing his nickname *Bendigo,* and a statue of him stands above the front entrance. He retired from the ring after winning, in forty-nine rounds, the All-England Championship in 1850, became a preacher and actually had an Australian town named after him.

Jack Russell at Swimbridge in North Devon recalls the fox-hunting clergyman who bred the original Jack Russell terrier. He died in 1883, aged eighty-eight.

Sir Tatton Sykes in Wolverhampton is named after the Yorkshire squire who rode in races when he was well over sixty and saw the St Leger run in seventy-six successive years, apart from missing one because of illness. He died in 1863, in his ninetieth year.

But the most celebrated all-round sportsman was George Osbaldeston (1786–1866), after whom an inn at Chipping Sodbury is called *The Squire*. Only five feet tall, he was foxhunter, cricketer, boxer, rowing champion, expert shot – and a legendary gambler. With it all he had the most perfect manners and temper!

The Malta at Batford, Harpenden, Herts, commemorates the heroism of the island's inhabitants during the Second World War.

OPPOSITE: *The Trafalgar at Harwich, Essex, spells out Nelson's famous message.*

20

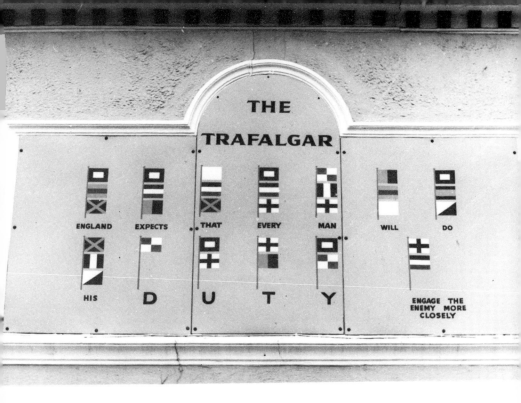

GREAT EVENTS AND OCCASIONS

Throughout the history of innkeeping, landlords with an eye to business have sought to make capital out of historic events by naming or renaming their houses accordingly.

There is *The Battle of Trafalgar* at Portslade in Sussex, and *The Battle of Waterloo* at Brighton. At Aldershot there is a pub named *The Heroes of Lucknow,* recalling the Indian Mutiny of 1857. *The Heroes of Alma* in St John's Wood, London and *The Heights of Alma* recall the first British victory in the Crimean campaign of 1854/5. *Mafeking Hero* at Bishop's Waltham, Hants, reminds us of that moment in 1900 when the news from South Africa sent England wild with relief and delight.

From the First World War come *General Allenby,* the hero of Palestine, Winterbourne Zelston, Dorset; *Earl Haig,* commander-in-chief of British Forces in France, Hounslow; and *Lord Gort,* Durham. Two VCs are *John Brunt* at Paddock Wood, Kent, and *Leefe Robinson* at Harrow Weald, Greater London. It was the latter who first shot down a Zeppelin, at nearby Cuffley in 1916.

Several licensed houses honour the fighting men of the Second World War: *The Red Beret,* Chelmsford, Essex; *The Parachute* at Henlow, Beds; *The Green Beret* at Walmer, Kent; *The Desert Rat* in Reigate, Surrey; and *The Battle of Britain* at Shears Green, Kent.

The Everest at Woodhouse, Sheffield; *The Summit* at Shirebrook, Notts; and *The Top of the World* at Warners End, Herts, all refer to the first ascent of Everest in 1953.

FAMOUS PEOPLE

It was once said that the true mark of renown in Britain was to be made the subject of a cartoon in *Punch,* but a more distinguished honour is to be made the subject of an inn sign. In the present century, however, this single honour is much rarer than it was in the nineteenth. The traveller journeys through the British countryside confronted on all sides by the names and faces of insignificant and forgotten Victorian servicemen, of minor reformers and meteoric politicians.

Here is a short 'Who's Who' of some of the more puzzling.

Duke of Cambridge. Grandson of George III, he was Commander-in-Chief of the British Army until the 1890s and a major opponent of military reform. Campbell-Bannerman insisted upon his ultimate resignation at the age of seventy-six.

Lord Raglan. The 'someone who blundered' from Tennyson's poem 'The Charge of the Light Brigade', Raglan was the British commander in the Crimea.

Sir Charles Napier. An inn at Chinnor, Oxon, is named after this hero of the Indian Mutiny.

Viscount Wolseley. He succeeded the Duke of Cambridge as Commander-in-Chief, after a brilliant career in most of the Victorian military campaigns in Africa. W. S. Gilbert wrote in *Patience* of 'the skill of Lord Wolseley in thrashing a cannibal', and in *The Pirates of Penzance* Grossmith, in the role of 'Major General Stanley' made himself up to look like Wolseley.

Marquis of Granby. John Manners (1721–70) was Commander-in-Chief during the Seven Years War and was beloved by his men for his courage, his honesty and his intolerance of corruption. It is said that he paid off his non-commissioned officers with a gratuity specifically to enable them to buy inns

to which to retire. Hence the popularity of the sign.

Lord Roberts. An inn in Sandy, Beds, recalls this Commander-in-Chief of the Indian Army, but his part in the Relief of Lucknow probably accounts for his appearance on signs.

Duke of York. Of 'ten thousand men' fame, he was the second and favourite son of George III, although his military prowess was undistinguished, as the old rhyme recalls.

Earl Howe. Admiral of the Fleet, he raised the siege of Gibraltar and arbitrated at the Portsmouth Mutiny in 1797, and is commemorated by the *Earl Howe* at Holmer Green, Bucks.

William Willett. He was a tireless advocate of the Daylight Saving scheme, which passed into law the year after his death, in 1916. The inn is at Petts Wood, Greater London.

Sir Rowland Hill. In 1840 his cherished idea of the Penny Post was put into operation: this became the envy of the whole world and is the reason why Britain remains the only country without a name of origin shown on her postage stamps.

Thomas Eldred. A master mariner (1586–1622) in the service of the East India Company, he was one of the first Englishmen to circumnavigate the globe and is remembered at Ipswich.

Jet and Whittle. At Podsmead, near Gloucester, this inn pays tribute to Sir Frank Whittle (born 1907), the pioneer of jet propulsion for aircraft.

Jenny Lind. Known the world over as 'The Swedish Nightingale', she reigned supreme as a singer during the middle years of the last century. She died in 1887 and inns at Sutton, Greater London, and Hastings are named after her.

Amy Johnson. The fearless and extremely popular aviator is remembered by *The Flying Eagle* in Edgware. She flew solo from England to Australia in

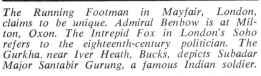

The Running Footman in Mayfair, London, claims to be unique. Admiral Benbow is at Milton, Oxon. The Intrepid Fox in London's Soho refers to the eighteenth-century politician. The Gurkha, near Iver Heath, Bucks, depicts Subadar Major Santabir Gurung, a famous Indian soldier.

1930 but lost her life in 1941 when flying as a pilot of the Air Transport Auxiliary over the Thames estuary.

Margaret Catchpole. Recalled at Ipswich, she was the heroine of the Rev. Richard Cobbold's biographical novel who risked her life for her smuggler lover and was eventually transported to Botany Bay.

Man of Ross. An inn at Ross-on-Wye is named after John Kyrle, a local benefactor who lived 1637–1724.

Thomas Lord. The founder of the famous cricket ground is honoured at West Meon in Hampshire.

Willie Wouldhave. At South Shields, this refers to a local man who discovered how to make a boat right itself if it capsized; the first lifeboat was built from this model in 1789 and kept at South Shields, where the first permanent lifeboat station was established.

The Oystermouth is at Swansea. The Wicked Lady is an apt name for an inn at Nomansland, near Wheathampstead, Herts. The Pineapple at Dorney, near Slough, recalls the first pineapple grown in England at Dorney Court. It was presented to Charles II.

A very short name for this inn at Cheriton, Hants.

COMIC AND CURIOUS SIGNS

One of the most appealing facets of inn signs is the unexpected sense of humour one so often comes across. A favourite is *The Quiet Woman* – shown variously as *The Good Woman* at Doncaster, *The Silent Woman,* at Cold Harbour, Dorset, or *The Headless Woman,* at Duddon in Cheshire. The *Nag's Head* at St Leonards, East Sussex, displays the portrait of a woman's head in a muzzle.

Not all the pungently satirical signs are directed at women. At King's Lynn a man in legal robes is shown carrying his head. The name of the inn is *The Honest Lawyer.*

A most original sign at Sutton, near Macclesfield, is that of *The Fool's Nook,* which shows a jester puzzling over an outsize egg apparently laid by a bird in a tree.

Similar zany humour is displayed in the signboard of *The Cuckoo Bush* at Gotham, Notts, where the men of this legendary village are endeavouring to keep the bird prisoner by erecting a fence of stakes around the tree in which it is perched!

Animal sociologists will be greatly interested in the reason behind the choice of name for *The Waltzing Weasel* at Birch Vale, Hayfield, in the Peak District. When the licensee was asked in 1965 by the local justices why she wished to change the name of the inn, she said: 'It sounds more rural in character, it has scientific foundation, and it's a far more entertaining title

25

The two sides of an inn sign in Tower Bridge Road, London.

than the present Birch Hall Inn.'

Many inn signs have a local curiosity as in *Doff Cockers* at Bolton. As 'cockers' were leather gaiters usually worn in times of snow, the name here was an invitation to customers to 'doff' (take off) their cockers and sit at ease in the bar parlour.

Other examples of local etymology are *The Wheal* (mine) at Cury, Cornwall; *The Finnygook* at Crafthole, Cornwall, where 'finny' indicates an old-time smuggler and 'gook' a ghost; and *The Scrogg* (thicket) in Newcastle upon Tyne.

A prize specimen is undoubtedly a public house in Stacey Close, Gravesend, Kent. It was built on the site of a maternity home destroyed in an air-raid during the last war and is called *The Stork at Rest.* The sign shows Doctor Stork reclining with drink and cigar.

Where would you like to live? *Home Sweet Home* at Roke, Oxon, and *Castle of Comfort,* near Priddy in Somerset, would surely appeal to you; or how about *Cottage of Content* at Carshalton, *Cottage by the Brook,* Stafford, and *Cottage in the Wood,* Burnley? There is also a *Custard House* at Small Heath, Birmingham, and a *Donkey House* at Windsor, where the barge donkeys were watered and their drivers beered!

For your table you might like to avail yourself of some *Rhubarb,* in Bristol, a *Sack of Potatoes,* Gosta

26

This is the delightful sign of The Welcome Stranger, Liverton, Devon.

THE STARVING RASCAL

QUIET WOMAN

The Starving Rascal at Amblecote, West Midlands, was named The Dudley Arms. Legend has it that a licensee once turned away a starving beggar, whose frozen body was found the next morning. Therefore the house became known as the Starver, and Courage has changed its name accordingly. The other side of the sign shows the beggar's ghost being welcomed by a new licensee.

The Quiet Woman is at Earl Sterndale, Derbyshire. The Boot is one of many pubs so called in north Bucks, recalling the legend of Sir John Shorn (see page 4).

At Beck Hole on the Yorkshire moors is a sign painted by Algernon Newton RA, who lived locally. The Hole in the Wall is at Richmond, Greater London, and in Cambridgeshire The Caxton Gibbet's sign swings only a few yards away from a replica of the original gibbet.

Green, Birmingham, or a *Bunch of Carrots,* Hampton Bishop, Herefs, and of course *The Devon Dumpling,* Shiphay, near Torquay, and *The Plum Pudding,* Armitage, Staffs, would come in very useful, with *The Stilton Cheese,* at Stilton, Cambs, and *The Bunch of Grapes,* Bridgwater, Somerset, to follow.

As for quenching a thirst, select from this excellent list: *Quart Pot,* Wickford, Essex: *Flowing Bowl,* Ramsgate: *Foaming Quart,* Burslem, Staffs: *Jug and Glass,* Langwith, Derbyshire, and *Comfortable Gill,* Stockport. If your friends are with you, bring in a *Butt of Ale,* Salisbury, a *Butt of Sherry,* Mere, Wiltshire, or a *Brandy Cask,* Pershore, Worcestershire.

29

The Castle and Ball is an unusual sign in Marlborough, Wilts. The Great White Horse in Ipswich, Suffolk, is the coaching inn where Mr Pickwick became involved with the lady with yellow curl papers. Dickens describes the sign as 'a stone statue of some rampacious animal with flowing mane and tail, distantly resembling an insane cart-horse'. The Bulldog in Oxford refers to the university officials responsible for maintaining discipline among the students. The Jack and Jill is at Coulsdon, Greater London.

THE JACK & JILL